HOW TO MAKE MONEY AS AN AUTHOR SELLING YOUR BOOKS ON AMAZON

25 MARKETING STRATEGIES TO GET IMMEDIATE BOOK SALES GUARANTEED

Christopher Mitchell

www.ChangeYourLifeOvernight.com

HOW TO MAKE MONEY AS AN AUTHOR SELLING YOUR BOOKS ON AMAZON! 25 MARKETING STRATEGIES TO GET IMMEDIATE BOOK SALES GUARNTEED!

Copyright © 2017 Christopher Mitchell

ISBN-13: 978-1544887852

ISBN-10: 154488785X

Printed In The United States Of America.

TABLE OF CONTENTS:

This book is a #1 Best-Seller for good reason: it teaches self-published authors how to increase their book sales in record time. Not only will this book teach you how to increase your book sales on Amazon, but it will also teach you how to move your books up the rankings on Amazon's Best-Sellers list. If you want to be known as an expert in your field, you not only have to write a book, but you must know how to market your book so that people can find it on Amazon among the millions of others. This is the book for you if you want to move your books up the Amazon rankings and get more sales. If you want to speak to Christopher, or perhaps join his team and have him become your personal mentor, you can contact him at his website below:

www.ChangeYourLifeOvernight.com

Chapter One:

Introduction

From 1996 to 2016, I was a health and fitness professional having operated my own personal training and nutritional consulting business. I enjoyed what I did for a living. I helped people change their lives. Teaching people how to eat healthy and workout correctly not only helped them lose weight and increase their confidence, but it helped them cure their cancer, diabetes, arthritis, joint pain, fibromyalgia, and multiple sclerosis to name a few. It was a rewarding career.

However, I was always limited to the number of people I could help because there are only twenty-four hours in a day. I can only meet with so many people at one time. This bothered me because I've always wanted to help millions of people all over the world, but physically training people in a gym all day long just wasn't going to allow that to happen. So, I started to pray and visualize on how I could reach more people. My favorite book, "The Holy Bible" gave me my answer on New Years of 2017.

Ask and it will be given to you; seek and you will find; knock and the door will be opened to you. **Matthew 7:7**

I asked God how I could reach and help more people change their lives all over the world and he answered me: **WRITE A BOOK!** I obeyed and the rest is history. That's why you're now reading this book. I had no idea when I wrote my first book, which was a weight loss book, that I would then be transitioning from a personal trainer to a published author who is now selling books all over the world. It's been quite a journey to say the least. It's been wonderful! I receive emails from people on a daily basis who have purchased my books from places I have never visited before in my life: The UK, China, India, Austria Germany, Australia, and Switzerland to name a few. My dream of helping people all over the world is coming true and it's all because I decided to write a book. The same thing can happen to you. You are an expert at something and you've also been through something in your life that can help others, if you're willing to write a book about it.

Pay very close attention to what you're about to read in the pages ahead. I have laid everything out for you in a very simple, easy to follow blueprint. This book will teach you exactly what to do and the order in which to do it. Absolutely anyone can learn how to sell books on Amazon if they'll simply follow the steps I'm about to reveal in this book.

Let me give you some factual statistics about how rare it is for you to become a published author and how big of an opportunity it is for you to start selling books on Amazon:

-Did you know that 99.75% of the people in the world have had a thought or a dream at some point in their lives to write a book, but less than 1% ever actually do? It's true!

-Out of the less than 1% who actually do write a book, only six out of every one thousand ever publish their book and sell a single copy.

-From this very small group of six out of every one thousand published authors, the average book only sells seventy-five copies in a lifetime.

As you can see from these mind boggling statistics, only about 0.00001% of the people in the world ever become a published author and sell at least seventy-five copies of a book. Instead of looking at this rare accomplishment as a bad thing, I encourage you to look at it as an amazingly huge opportunity for you to cash in on. This statistic doesn't exist because it's extremely hard to reach this accomplishment, but rather because so many people in the world today give up before they ever even start. Your competition is so small because there's so few people actually writing books. Just by taking action will put you in the top 1% of over achievers in the entire world.

That's something to get excited about! When I published my first book as a completely brand new, unknown author, I sold more than seventy-five copies the very first week. That's crazy to think about! However, if I can do it then you can too. Just follow the steps in this book and you can get the same results.

This book is strictly about how to market your books to bring in sales and reviews on Amazon. If you have not yet published your first book then this book is a little ahead of where you need to be. You first need to write and publish a book in order for this book to make sense. Please get my other book and read it first. It will teach you exactly how to write your first book and get it up on Amazon. It's titled: **SELL YOUR FIRST BOOK!** It's available on Amazon here: www.amazon.com/author/fitchristophermitchell

Chapter Two:

How To Upload To Amazon

This exact chapter is also in my first book **SELL YOUR FIRST BOOK**, but I've included it in this book as well, just in case you didn't read my first book. If you've already published your book on Amazon then use this chapter as a refresher course. You might learn something here that makes you realize you didn't upload your book correctly the first time. By changing a few things inside your Kindle Direct Publishing and Create Space accounts it could dramatically increase your book sales. Let's begin!

The first website that you're going to use is called: www.createspace.com

Create Space is owned by Amazon. Create Space is going to act like your publishing agent. You're going to go through Create Space to get your book up on Amazon in the paperback format. It's a really simple process and you're going to wish you would have written a book a long time ago once you see how truly easy it is. Your book is about to be seen on the biggest book selling platform in the entire world. Follow these exact steps in this order and then you'll be set up for success:

-Go to www.createspace.com and create a new account. It's 100% free.

-Once you have created your account click on **Add New Title**.

-Write in **The Title** of your book.

-Click **Paperback** option.

-Click **Get Started** to the right of the Guided option.

-The next process is the **Title Information**. Fill in The Title, The Subtitle, Author Name, and choose The Language you want your book to be printed in. Click Save & Continue.

-Now you're going to have an **ISBN** number created for your book. Choose to have Create Space create a brand new ISBN number for you for free. Click Save & Continue.

-Once your ISBN numbers are created for you go back inside your Microsoft Word document and add them to the second page of your book under the copyright logo. You can refer to the second page of this book to see. It should appear like this:

Copyright © 2017 Christopher Mitchell

ISBN-13: 978-1542575706

ISBN-10: 1542575702

-Save your Microsoft Word document again and now your book will have your ISBN numbers included.

-Now you're going to choose the **Interior** format for your book. Where it says Interior Type choose **Black & White**.

-Now you're going to choose the **Trim Size** of your book. This should be either **5x8** or **6x9** unless you created a different dimension for your book inside of Microsoft Word. These two sizes are the most popular and offer you the widest distribution options for your book to be sold on Amazon.

-Now you get to fill in information about you, your book, the price you want to sell your book for, and the distribution channels you want to sell your book on. Fill in the **Description** for your book and the **Bio About The Author** with good, detailed information about you and your book. This information will show up on Amazon alongside your book.

If you want to get an idea of how this appears on Amazon do a search on either my name or the title of my book and you can see what mine looks like. Type either of these phrases in on Amazon and my book will come up for you to see:

1. Christopher Mitchell

2. Sell Your First Book!

You also get to decide on the price you want to sell your book for. I personally encourage you to sell your paperback book anywhere between **$9.99** and **$15.99** depending on the need for your book and the amount of pages that your book has. Just so you know, you'll earn more money from your Kindle eBooks than you will from your paperback books. If you sell your paperback book for $15.99 you will get paid $7.44 per copy. So, it's not quite 50% royalty. Kindle will pay you 70% royalty for each sale. The more you charge for your book the more you'll make. However, you don't want to be greedy and charge too much or people won't buy your book at all. Focus on selling a lot of books for a little bit of profit and the money will start to add up to big amounts.

-Now you **Upload Your Book File** from your Microsoft Word Document that you just saved with your new ISBN numbers. Click Save & Continue.

-Then you're going to **Upload The Print Ready PDF Cover** for your book. Click Save & Continue.

-Choose whether you want your cover to be **Matte** or **Glossy** finish. Click Save & Continue.

-Now you're going to complete the setup by **submitting your files for review**.

Create Space will get back to you within twenty-four hours. They're either going to tell you to change something if you did something wrong or they'll ask you to look over the finished proof and either accept it or deny it. If you like the finished look accept it. Once you accept the way your book looks it will be live on Amazon and any other distribution channels you selected within twenty-four hours at the most. Every single one of my books went up live on Amazon within twenty-four hours of accepting the proof.

Once you finish this process you then want to submit your book to Kindle Direct Publishing so that it can be sold as a digital download, also known as an eBook. Kindle will make up 50-85% of all your book sales.

Follow these exact steps in this order and then you'll be set up for success:

--Go to http://kdp.amazon.com and create a new account. It's 100% free.

-Underneath "Create A New Title" click on **Kindle eBook**.

-Enter your **Book Title** and **Subtitle**.

-Skip past Series and Edition Number.

-Enter the **Author Name**.

-Enter a detailed **Description** of what your book is about.

-Click on: **I own the copyright and I hold the necessary publishing rights**.

-Enter **seven specific keywords** that describe what your book is about. These keywords will help buyers find your book in the search results.

-Choose the **Categories** that your book represents. You want to be very selective here. You don't necessarily want to choose the most obvious categories and let me tell you why. My first book that I ever wrote was a weight loss book. The weight loss niche is a huge category. Since I was a brand new, unknown author it would have been very stupid for me to put my book in the general weight loss category. Why? Well, because there is a ton of competition in weight loss. So, what I decided to do in this scenario is choose a smaller, more focused category like diet, nutrition, and vitamins. This would have a lot less competition, which would give me a much better chance of getting my book to the number one ranking in my book categories. The only thing that matters on Amazon is getting your book ranked number one.

-Scroll down to where it says Pre-order and click: **I am ready to release my book now**.

-Click Save and Continue.

-Underneath **enable DRM on this Kindle eBook** click No. By clicking "no" it will enable you to make a lot more money in the long run.

-**Upload eBook Manuscript** from your Microsoft Word Document.

-Upload your **5x8 JPG** front cover.

-Click Save and Continue.

-Click **All Territories**.

-Underneath **Royalty and Pricing** click on **35%**.

-Make the price of your book **$0.99**.

-Scroll down and click **Publish Your Kindle eBook**.

The reason you set the price of your book at only $0.99 is because your book is brand new and no one knows about it yet. You need to get ten sales and ten customer reviews as fast as humanly possible. At only $0.99 you can contact your closest friends and family members and ask them to do you a favor. Ask them to buy your book. Since it's only $0.99 they shouldn't mind helping you out. Ask them to wait for one hour after they buy your book and then leave you a five star customer review.

These sales and reviews will help your book to immediately spike the Amazon algorithm, which will increase the ranking of your book in your categories dramatically. Once your book starts climbing the Amazon charts making its way toward the number one ranking, which is the goal for any book, you can then raise the price of your book. I recommend keeping the price of your Kindle eBook at $3.99 or less. If you set the price higher than this most people probably won't buy it. At $3.99 you'll earn $2.77 of that amount for each copy that you sell.

If you want to become a published author, but don't actually want to write your book, I do offer a service as a ghost writer. My ghost writing service includes writing your book, editing your book, full cover design, and publishing your book on Amazon in paperback and Kindle formats. If you're interested in this service, feel free to email me on my website. www.ChangeYourLifeOvernight.com

Chapter Three:

Amazon's Algorithm

In my personal opinion, this is the most important chapter of the book. If you want to become a successful author you need to spend more time studying and mastering Amazon's algorithm than you do trying to write the perfect masterpiece. Some of the worst written books become number one best sellers, while some of the best written books never even sell a single copy. Have you ever wondered why this is? I'm going to explain the answer to you in this chapter now.

In one single word the answer is "marketing". However, let me teach you the actual details. The better answer is learning how Amazon's algorithm works and using it to your advantage to increase book sales.

The main goal for every published author who is selling their books on Amazon should be to get their books to the number one ranking in the categories that the books are listed in. It should be no surprise that the higher your books are ranked means the more your books will sell. The problem with this is that a lot of the books that make their way to the number one ranking spent a lot of money on marketing to get there. For most brand new authors, the last thing they have is a lot of money. So, learning what I share with you in the next few chapters will benefit you greatly.

Believe it or not, Amazon's algorithm is actually quite simple. I'm going to explain what you need to know in a very easy to understand manner right now. Once you learn these things you simply have to keep repeating them with every new book you publish.

1. Each time your book receives a sale or download it counts as one point toward the ranking of your book.

2. Each day, the previous day's score is cut in half and is then added to the points your book receives today.

3. Every book on Amazon is ranked by its current score in every category. Let me give you an example:

On Monday, my book sells 20 copies. That's 20 points towards its ranking.

On Tuesday, my book sells 40 copies. Those 40 points are added to half of Monday's total, which is 10 points. Add 10 points to 40 points, which equals 50 points for today.

On Wednesday, my book sells 56 copies. Those 56 points are added to half of Tuesday's total, which is 25 points. Add 25 points to 56 points, which equals 81 points for today.

This is easy to understand, but there are things about this process that contribute to the unexplainable behavior of the algorithm. Your sales rank is relative to other books. As your book is moving up the rankings it is pushing other books down the rankings. If other books are moving up the rankings Amazon's algorithm is pushing your book down the rankings. The more recent a book has a sale means the more that book moves up the rankings.

Because of books having recent sales it will quickly knock your book down the rankings, even if your book just had a lot of sales the day before. Amazon's algorithm prefers a book that has lower, but steady sales, than a book that has a lot of sales on one day, but no sales after that. Let me give you an example:

Let's take two different books in the same category. Book number one receives exactly ten sales per day, but these sales come in day after day for three weeks straight. However, book number two decides to do a one day promotion and spikes the algorithm tremendously by receiving three hundred sales in a single day. The next day the book gets zero sales.

At the end of a three week period book number one has a total of 210 sales, while book number two has 300 sales. Book number one has a much higher sales ranking even though it sold 90 copies less than book number two because the algorithm recognizes that it is making consistent sales every single day, while book number two hasn't made a single sale in three weeks. This makes book number two drop off the charts nowhere to be found.

To become a successful author, you want to think of getting sales as a marathon, not a sprint. Focus on getting consistent sales for your book over the long run, rather than getting a lot of sales in one single day.

The ranking of your book on Amazon is determined by the number of sales and downloads it receives and nothing else. Your book's ranking is not affected when you get a bad rating or customer review. Not by Amazon's algorithm anyway. However, a bad rating or customer review could keep other people from buying your book, which will result in lost sales. The only thing you want to focus on is getting consistent sales and downloads for your book. If you do, Amazon's algorithm will love you, which will result in your book moving up the rankings.

You need to make twice as many sales to move your book up the rankings than you need to make to maintain your book's ranking. For example, you may need to get 40 sales per day to hit a given rank, but once that momentum is created you will only need 20 sales per day to maintain that rank. However, if zero sales are made for your book on any given day your book's score will be cut in half on the next day.

Have you ever wondered how a book could reach the number one best sellers list, but the book hasn't even been released yet? Pre-orders are counted on the day the book is ordered, rather than the date of the book's actual release. This explains how a book that has not yet been released can reach the top of the charts. Now that you know how Amazon's algorithm works you can use it to your advantage. Let's recap:

-It takes twice as many sales to reach a certain rank as it does to stay there.

-Your book's ranking will change on a daily basis due to the performance of other books.

-A book that is ranked higher than your book does not mean that it has more overall sales.

-To stay at the top of the rankings it's better for your book to get just a few, but consistent sales every single day of the week, rather than to get a lot of sales in one single day.

-Pre-orders increase your book's rankings and can get you to the top of the charts even though your book hasn't been released yet.

-Kindle Unlimited downloads increase your book's ranking even if the book never gets read.

-Book rankings change on a daily basis. So, it's never too late for your book to become a number one best seller on Amazon.

I hope you now understand how Amazon's algorithm works. In the up coming chapters, I'm going to share with you some different things you can do to increase your sales and rankings. The main thing you need to remember is to do these things I'm about to teach you on a regular, consistent basis, rather than doing them just one time to get a big spike in the algorithm.

Chapter Four:

Customer Reviews

I'm going to be sharing some promotional websites with you coming up. These websites market your book to legitimate lists of book buyers. These websites will get you sales for your books guaranteed. However, most of these websites have certain criteria that your book must meet in order for them to promote your book. The main criteria is having ten customer reviews for your books on Amazon. So, the very first thing you must do for every single book you publish is to get ten sales and ten reviews immediately. I'm going to show you how to get these ten sales and ten reviews for your book right now! Continue on to the next page and learn exactly what I do every time I publish a new book.

As soon as I publish a new book, which is every single week, I contact two sets of people and ask them to do me a HUGE favor. I tell them that I just published my newest book and I need to get ten sales and ten reviews immediately so that I can launch my book to the world publicly. The first group of people is my closest friends and family members; the people who would do anything for me.

The second group of people that I contact is other self-published authors I met on Facebook. We help each other get legitimate sales and reviews for our books. Any time a self-published author tells me that they just published a new book, I immediately go onto Amazon and buy it. I then read it and leave them a five star customer review. They turn around and return the favor when I publish a new book.

When you ask your friends and family members to buy your book and leave you a customer review, make sure they do indeed **buy** your book and not just leave you a customer review. When someone buys your book the customer review will come up as **verified**. When they leave you a customer review without buying your book it will not be verified, which tells professionals it's not a real review. Amazon knows it's not a legitimate review too. A verified review will increase your rankings.

Here is my basic email/text message that I send to people when I publish a brand new book and need to get my ten sales and ten reviews. You're welcome to copy it and use it:

Hi (name), I just released my brand new book! The title of the book is: **SELL YOUR FIRST BOOK!** I'm trying to increase my rankings on Amazon. I need to get ten sales and ten reviews by midnight tonight. Would you mind doing me a HUGE favor please? I've set the price at a promotional bargain of only $0.99. Would you mind buying the book for me and then leave me a good five star customer review an hour later please? It will only take you thirty seconds to buy it and it will help me out tremendously. It would mean the world to me. All you have to do is click on this link right here to get the book:

www.amazon.com/author/fitchristophermitchell

I want to share some important key points with you about customer reviews that you need to know ahead of time. This will definitely save you frustration down the road.

-In order for someone to leave you a customer review on your book, they must have already spent at least $50 on Amazon at some point.

-Tell the person who buys your book to wait at least an hour after they buy it before they leave you the review.

-Tell the person who buys your book not to mention anything about their personal relationship with you. Tell the person to keep their review strictly about the book and not about you personally. Otherwise, Amazon will delete it.

-You cannot have someone who is connected to you in any way leave you a review. This includes someone who lives at the same physical address that you live at, someone using the same computer (IP address) that you use, and someone who may have bought something from Amazon and had it shipped to your address.

-You will at some point get a negative review. Don't worry about it too much though. Yes, a negative review could keep some people from buying your book, but it will not affect the ranking of your book. You cannot get rid of a negative review unless you can prove to Amazon that the person who left it is purposefully trying to damage your name and reputation.

I have a stalker who did this to me two days in a row. This person made up lies about me, said cuss words, and even made sexual remarks about me. I told Amazon what was going on and they removed the reviews.

All of my books are listed on my social media pages with the Amazon link attached to them. Follow these easy steps to give your friends and family your book link:

-Go to Amazon and do a search for your name in the search bar.

-Click on the Kindle book link, **NOT** the paperback book link. There are two separate links so make sure you give them the Kindle link. Once your Kindle book comes up, copy the entire link in the website search bar at the top of the page.

-Go to www.bitly.com

-Paste your link in the empty space and click shorten.

-Send them that shortened link.

Chapter Five:

Book Giveaway Promotion

Yes, it's exactly what it sounds like. You're going to give your book away for free. When I first heard about what I'm going to share with you I said, heck no! I became an author so I could sell my books and make money, not give them away for free. Is that thought going through your mind right now too? If it is, don't worry. It's going to pay off in a big way.

However, in order for this marketing tactic to work I feel that you need to have at least one of two things, but it would be better if you have both:

1. Have multiple books for sale.

2. Have your contact information listed in your book.

Let me explain more in detail. When you do a free book giveaway it's quite obvious that you will not be making any money from these books. However, that's not the reason for doing a free book giveaway. The number one reason for giving your book away for free is to hope that it will pay off big time down the road.

Allow me to open your mind to a new dimension of thinking. I have multiple books published that sell all over the world. However, if you're a brand new author publishing your first book don't let this bother you. Everyone, including myself, were also first time authors at one point. Now that I do have many different books for sale, let me tell you the reasoning behind a free book giveaway.

You decide to give away one of your books for free. Just so you know, a free book giveaway only lasts for a day or two. The reason why you give away a free book for a day or two is to get a lot of people to find out who you are. When you're an unknown author a lot of people won't spend money buying your book because they don't know you or if your book is any good. They don't want to take a risk on you even though the cost of your book may only be a dollar. On the other hand, when your book is absolutely free any one will grab a copy because they have nothing to lose if your book isn't any good.

However, if you give your book away for free and a lot of people download it some of them will actually read it. Of those who read it some of them will like it. These people are why you do the free giveaway in the first place. Now, you just got a new fan. Here's how this could benefit you:

-If you have other books for sale this person could immediately go buy those books. This has happened to me on many different occasions. See, that free book giveaway is paying off.

-This person could loan your book out to a friend or family member that they know. If the friend or family member likes your book then that person could become a new fan. This process could then repeat all over again many times over. See, that free book giveaway is paying off.

-This person might be rich, famous, or have a lot of influence. This person could contact you personally and offer you a speaking engagement that pays big bucks. See, that free book giveaway is paying off.

-This person might have a financial opportunity for you to partner with them in business. See, that free book giveaway is paying off.

-This person might be a Hollywood film maker and want to turn your book into a blockbuster film. That's exactly what happened to the book **"The Shack"**, which is a self-published book and has sold more than twenty million copies. See, that free book giveaway is paying off.

These are only a few of the many ways that giving your book away for free could pay off in a big way. Believe me, these things happen to authors around the world every single day. Now you just need to have faith and believe that these things will happen to you. I'm believing for lucrative speaking engagements.

I'm believing that a Hollywood film producer is going to turn my book **"My Inspiring True Life Story"** into the next blockbuster film of the year. I'm believing that my books are going to change people's lives and these people are going to send me huge amounts of cash to thank me for sharing my knowledge with them. I'm believing that huge doors are opening for me because of my books.

So, hopefully now you can see why it would benefit you to give away your book for free. It might be free temporarily, but one big connection could pay you back a million times over for the free books that you give away. Just remember this:

The law of sowing and reaping states that whatever you sow you will reap. This law can also be interpreted as giving and receiving. If you bless someone with a free book something good will come back to you. It has to.

Now, let me teach you how to properly set up your free book giveaway. Follow these exact steps and your free book giveaway will be a huge success for you.

-Login to your Kindle account.

-Click on Promote and Advertise to the right of the book that you want to give away for free.

-Click on Free Book Promotion.

-Click the button that says Create a new Free Book Promotion.

-Enter the start date of when you want your free book giveaway to start.

-Enter the end date of when you want your free book giveaway to end.

-Click on Save Changes.

A few hours before your free book giveaway promotion starts raise the price of your Kindle eBook several dollars. I usually raise the price of my Kindle eBook to $9.99. The reason I do this is because when the free book giveaway begins, Amazon will do a price slash. This means they put a slash through the price of your book. In this case, Amazon will put a slash through the $9.99. Right below the $9.99 the price will show up for free, but it will also show the customer that they just saved $9.99. This gives the customer more perceived value for the book and makes them appreciate the amazing deal they just received a whole lot more.

I want to share something with you that I didn't know. You're allowed five free book giveaway days every ninety days. So, use your five free days the best that you can. If you only want to use one free day then your start and end date will be the same exact day on the calendar. It's a full twenty-four hour period. So, that's how you properly set up your free book giveaway. You can choose to use one free day per week for five weeks or you can use all five days right in a row. How you decide to use your free book giveaway promotion days are totally up to you.

However, this next marketing tactic I'm going to share with you is a very strategic way to increase your sales, so pay close attention. I like to use my free book giveaways one at a time. I use one free day each week for five weeks rather than using all five of my free days in a row. The reason for this is because it allows me to use this secret five different times compared to if I used all five of my free days in a row, which would only allow me to use this secret once. Here's my personal secret that I'm talking about.

On the last day of your free book giveaway promotion or on the same day if you're only running a one day promotion, you need to login to your Kindle account and do two separate things at 6:00 pm est.

1. **Cancel** your free book promotion. By canceling your promotion, it will turn the promotion off. You cancel it by going through the same steps as you did when you set up the free promotion. However, this time instead of setting up a promotion, you simply cancel the promotion that is currently running.

2. After you cancel the promotion, you need to immediately change the price of your Kindle eBook to **$0.99**.

All of the traffic that you're driving to your book for the free giveaway will be scattered all over the world, meaning different time zones. 6:00 pm est. means it's only 3:00 pm pst. When you make a change to your Kindle account it takes on average about three hours for the change to go into effect. So, by the time the change happens, it will be around 9:00 pm on the east coast, but only 6:00 pm on the west coast.

Amazon is based on the west coast. This means that all of their daily updates and promotions stop at 12:00 am pst. So, when you cancel your promotion and change the price to $0.99 at 6:00 pm est, by the time the change takes place, it will give you three more hours on the east coast and six more hours on the west coast. The places where I'm going to show you to promote your free book giveaway at are sending traffic to your free book giveaway until 12:00 am pst. These websites don't know that you changed your price from free to $0.99. So, they keep sending you traffic. The traffic is under the impression that they're going to get your book for free, but when they get to your book they'll find out that the price is $0.99. They realized they missed the cut off time for your free promotion. However, $0.99 isn't a lot of money, so some of the people will go ahead and actually buy your book.

This is huge for you. Not only did you get a lot of free books out for the day, which could potentially bring you all kinds of opportunities in the future, but the last few hours of the night you're going to get paid sales as well. This will boost the ranking of your book tremendously. So, even though you ran a free promotion for the day, it will actually end with paid sales. This is a nice little marketing secret that can bring you paid sales, increase your ranking, and allow you to take advantage of the traffic that you generated for the free book giveaway promotion. However, you must remember to cancel the promotion at 6:00 pm est and change the price of your book to $0.99.

If you use this marketing secret on a regular, weekly basis like I do, it can steadily increase the ranking of your book and eventually get your book to the top of the charts. That should be every authors marketing game plan. Now that you understand the strategy behind giving your book away for free, do you see how a free book giveaway promotion could actually pay you for a long time to come? See, that free book giveaway is paying off.

Chapter Six:

Free Marketing Strategies

When I first started writing and publishing books I was dead broke. I barely had money to buy food with, let alone have money to spend on marketing my books. So, I had to learn some creative ways to increase sales for my books. These creative ways, which are completely FREE, are what I'm going to teach you about in this chapter now.

1. **Publish a new book every 90 days**. If you thought you were just going to write one book and become a millionaire, think again. You have a better chance of getting struck by lightning. In chapter three, I taught you about Amazon's algorithm and publishing a new book every 30-90 days will give you an edge above

most of the other authors. Every time you publish a new book you get five free days to run promotions for your book. However, you can only use these five free days every ninety day period. So, by publishing a new book at least every ninety days, you can use these five free days to boost your downloads. I personally publish a brand new book every single week.

The more people you have that download your books, the more people will get to know you as an author and the more potential referrals you'll receive. These things will keep your books and your name as an author fresh in the minds of book readers, ultimately making more people search for you, which will make Amazon's algorithm come across you more often, resulting in more book sales.

2. **Write 100 page books**. If you were thinking that there is absolutely no way you could ever publish a new book every ninety days, let alone every single week like I do, I'm here to tell you that you most certainly can. Your goal is to only write 100 page books. That is how you accomplish this goal. The authors who make the most money selling books are the ones who publish new books on a regular and consistent basis. Statistics prove that 90% of all book buyers never even read past the first chapter. So, that's an even more important reason to keep your books short. By keeping your books short, you'll be able to publish more books on a regular basis, you'll make a lot more money, and the buyers will actually read them. If you have books that are several hundred pages long, break them down into several books.

3. **Ask for a review in your book**. I have a page that asks the reader to please leave me a five star customer review on Amazon. This will absolutely get you more customer reviews for your books. A customer review is a form of marketing. Some people will only buy something if it has good reviews, but most people will never even think of leaving you a review for your book. They have way more important things to think about than to write a customer review for your book.

Before I learned this marketing strategy, I had never before in my entire life left an author a review for their book. However, I also never had an author ask me to leave them a review either. If an author would have asked me in their book to leave them a good review, I would have gladly done so.

Just like I mentioned in the beginning of this book, The Holy Bible says this:

Ask and it will be given to you; seek and you will find; knock and the door will be opened to you. **Matthew 7:7**

However, guess what else it says in The Holy Bible in another verse:

You do not have because you do not ask God. **James 4:2**

So, it obviously pays to ask. I know for a fact that by asking my readers to leave me a review that's the only reason why some of them leave me one. It looks good for your book when you have a lot of five star customer reviews, and again, you have to remember that some people will only buy things that have a lot of reviews. Here's exactly what I ask for in every single one of my books. You can copy this if you want to.

After you read this book, would you mind doing me a huge favor please? Would you be kind enough to write me a five star customer review for this book on Amazon? By giving this book a good review it will help me as an author and help this book move up the rankings on Amazon. Your words have power. If you wouldn't mind supporting this book, I would be extremely grateful. I would love to hear your feedback. You're welcome to contact me at me personal website anytime. I wish you the very best of success in every area of your life.

Sincerely,
Christopher Mitchell
www.ChangeYourLifeOvernight.com

4. **Mention your other books**. You'll notice when you finish reading this book on the very last page I let the reader know that I have other books available along with my author link. This makes it easy for them to simply click on the book of their choice if they're interested in another book that I have to offer. This FREE and very tiny strategy has increased sales for me. I can only imagine how many book sales I would have lost or would continue to lose in the future simply by leaving this last page out of my books. Make sure you don't overlook something so simple.

5. **Keyword optimization**. This is completely FREE, but can have a huge effect on your sales, ranking, and visibility. Inside your Create Space and Kindle accounts is where you submit the keywords for your books. You need to really study what words

you should submit because they could make or break the ranking for your book. You want to focus on keywords that don't have a lot of competition. Test out single keywords as well as phrases. To do this manually type in words into Amazon's search bar and wait a second before you press enter. Amazon will autofill different phrases underneath what you just typed in. Amazon is really helping you here. Whatever Amazon fills in is what is most searched for. Those are the words and phrases you want to use as keywords for your book.

The five places Amazon's algorithm is searching for keywords is your Title, Subtitle, Description, Back Cover, and Customer Reviews. The number one place to put in optimized keywords is your Title. Keywords that you use in your title will show up in the URL for your book making it easier for your title to show up in searches for those words. Your goal is to have your book rank in the top three search results for a specific keyword or phrase. The top three search results are where 90% of all book sales are made.

The second most important place for optimized keywords is in the book description. In the very first sentence of your book description is also the perfect place to mention accolades and comparables. If you or your book have won any awards be sure to mention that in the description of your book. Anything and everything is worth mentioning. Brag about your accolades in this area.

Next is mentioning a **comparable**. A comparable is language that compares your title to best-selling authors and titles. This will let fans of

those popular authors know that they should check your book out next. A comparable is when you mention something along the lines of:
If you like "The Whole30" **then you'll love** "How To Lose Weight With Intermittent Fasting".

6. **Enroll your book in KDP Select**. This is Amazon's exclusive loyalty program for authors. There are several benefits that come with KDP Select, including Kindle Countdown Deals and Kindle Free Days. Your book will also be included in the Kindle Unlimited program. By enrolling your book in KDP Select you'll receive 70% commissions in markets that only pay 35% to authors who are not enrolled. If you don't change the settings that are already set, every new book you publish is automatically enrolled. Login to your Kindle account to read all the details

about enrolling your book in KDP Select and its benefits.

7. **Create your Author Central page.** This is a FREE gift to you from Amazon, but a lot of authors don't take advantage of it. To create your FREE account, go to this link: https://authorcentral.amazon.com

Your Author Central page gives you the following benefits as an author:

-Allows you to write a bio about yourself as an author so people on Amazon can get to know you.

-Allows you to connect your Kindle book with your Paperback book so people know that you have both formats to choose from. Amazon will encourage them to buy both and give them a discount for doing so.

-Allows you to bring all of your books together in one place so people who come across one of your books can very easily find out you have others.

-Allows people who buy and enjoy your books to become your followers. Every single time you publish a new book Amazon will alert your followers and let them know about it. This is FREE marketing for you.

8. **Use Social Media**. There are so many social media platforms out there today you have to choose the one or two that you have the biggest following on. The most well known social media platforms to market your books on are:

-Twitter

-LinkedIn

-YouTube

-Facebook

-Instagram

I personally use Facebook and YouTube the most, but you can use any website you feel is best for you and your type of book. Whichever social media website you decide to use for marketing, make sure you carry yourself like a professional and don't get annoying with your posts like an amateur would. If you annoy people, not only will they pass on getting your book, but they will more than likely delete you or block you from their page altogether.

On Facebook, you can post your book link from Amazon and tag your closest friends and family members. If they accept the tag and allow it to show up on their wall, then all of their friends and family members on Facebook can see the post as well. This is another way of getting FREE marketing for your book.

Another thing that I recommend you do on Facebook is join a bunch of different groups. Groups are FREE to be a part of and you can post your link to your book on Amazon. I encourage you to join groups for authors and groups that your book would give people a solution for. I'm a part of several weight loss groups because I have a book on weight loss. This is another way of getting FREE marketing for your book.

9. **Create your Goodreads page**. This is a FREE gift to you, but a lot of authors don't take advantage of it. To create your FREE account, go to this link: www.goodreads.com

Goodreads is the world's largest website for book readers and book recommendations. It's like a large library that you can wander through and see everyone's bookshelves, their reviews, and their ratings. You can also post your own reviews and catalog what books you've read.

The Goodreads Author Program allows published authors to claim their profile page to promote their books and engage with readers. Once verified, your author profile page will include the official Goodreads Author badge, which you can use to tell your fans to follow you on Goodreads.

The website receives an unbelievable 45 million visitors every month. So, the exposure you can get as an author is absolutely unbeatable. The more books you have published the better the website can work for you. The website will put you in touch with a lot of people and it can open up a lot of doors for you. Get started on this website immediately!

You can also advertise and promote your books with paid advertising campaigns to targeted book buyers. This website has opened a lot of doors for a lot of authors and it could very well do the same for you. Create your profile and learn your way around. This is another way of getting FREE marketing for your book.

If you're a brand new author and do not have a lot of disposable cash laying around for marketing, then use the strategies I just gave you in this chapter. Over the long term, these strategies could sell a lot of books and make you a lot of money, but only if you're consistent with your marketing efforts. Remember that consistency is the key to becoming a successful author.

Chapter Seven:

Paid Marketing Strategies

Most people in the world dream of writing a book, but very few ever will. Of the very few who do write a book only a tiny fraction of those will ever publish their book. Of the minuscule few who do publish their book most of them will never sell a single copy of their book. So, as you can see, for a person to write a book, publish their book, and then go on to sell copies of their book puts that person in a very rare, elite category of individuals.

Why is this percentage of people so small when so many people around the world have this dream? In my opinion the reason why is paid marketing. Most people don't even think it's possible to write and publish a book, let alone sell millions of copies and become wealthy as a published author. Their belief systems are so negative that they talk themselves out of even pursuing their dream in the first place. For the very elite few who do write and publish a book their belief systems are still so negative that they only think of writing as a hobby. They don't believe that they could ever become a successful author who could earn millions of dollars selling books. That belief system is what keeps them from taking the action I'm going to share with you in this chapter, which is the most important action that a person needs to take in order to become a successful author.

That action I'm referring to is paid marketing. Most authors will never spend a dime on marketing their book because they don't believe that their book will ever become a number one best seller. That's why so few books ever sell a single copy. It's a lack of faith. When my Heavenly Father told me to write a book, not only was I 100% obedient, but I told myself that if I'm going to become an author then I'm going to do whatever it takes to become successful, no matter what I have to do.

My wife was in absolute agreement with me. We studied marketing strategies around the clock. We sold practically everything we owned, including our only car, which was paid for in order to have money to market our books. We believed in ourselves and the calling that God gave us. Throughout our research and study time we learned some things that separate the successful authors from everyone else. The successful authors were willing to pay the price, the wannabe's weren't.

We found out that most authors who became number one best sellers **bought** their way there. They were willing to spend whatever amount of money they needed to in order to get their book to number one. Publishing a book is a business. Business is about one thing and one thing only, and that is making money. Most of the Christian Pastors even know this.

Famous authors like Joel Osteen, Joyce Meyer, TD Jakes, and the list continues, understand that in order to sell books to people around the world requires that they spend money on marketing their books. A lot of big name authors use a company called Result Source.

Pastor Mark Driscoll contracted the company Result Source to place his book Real Marriage on The New York Times Best Seller List for a $200,000 fee. To achieve this, the contract stated that Result Source would purchase at least 11,000 copies of his book in one week. This took place and his book successfully reached number one on the hardcover advice bestseller list on January 22, 2014.

Despite not having $200,000 to pay for that kind of marketing, most authors never even spend a dime on marketing their books. The reason why is because they don't see any value investing in their book because they don't believe in their book. Pastor Mark Driscoll obviously believed in his book and that is why he invested so much money into it.

In order for you to become successful you need to believe in your book too. Are you going to spend a hundred dollars a week going out to eat, or are you going to sacrifice that time with your friends and invest that money in marketing your book instead? The answer you give to that question will determine whether you're going to become a successful author or not.

My wife Stacy and I had a Lexus that was paid for. So, I told her that I wanted to sell the car for some cash so that we could invest it into our new business. Without skipping a beat, she told me she agreed. When people found out what we did to follow our dream they told us we were the stupidest people they had ever known. Stacy's mom and dad told us that was the dumbest thing that we ever did. They ridiculed us like there was no tomorrow. However, they lack vision, my wife and I don't. Again, my favorite book, The Holy Bible says:

Where there is no vision, the people perish. **Proverbs 29:18** KJV.

They can't see what we see. They can't see themselves helping millions of people around the world change their lives. My wife and I can. So, we followed our heart and we're willing to do whatever it takes to succeed as authors. Unless you feel the same way about yourself you will never succeed. You must be willing to invest money in marketing if you want your books to sell.

I understand if you don't have an extra hundred thousand dollars laying around that you can dish out for marketing. Trust me, most authors don't and never will. However, you don't need a lot of money to market your books. You just need a little bit, but you need to market your books consistently. Consistent sales is the number one thing that's going to get your book to the top of the rankings.

My wife and I have studied for countless hours, days, and weeks putting together the following list of promotional websites to help you market your books and bring in sales. I've put the list in order from least expensive to most expensive and I've also included some info about what kind of sales you can expect to receive by making each investment.

So, here are the best promotional websites that I have personally used to market your books and bring in sales. Whichever websites you decide to use to bring in sales remember that your marketing efforts must be consistent and ongoing, not a one time thing. Rome wasn't built in a day and neither is a huge book publishing empire. Do the things I'm sharing with you in this book on a consistent basis and in time you can become a best-selling author. I believe in you!

1. www.fiverr.com/bknights
This guy is the best investment you can ever make for only $5. I use him every time I publish a brand new book. He will promote your book for either a free promotion or a paid $0.99 promotion. When I use him I average 250-500 downloads for a free promotion, and 10-20 sales for a paid promotion. This is a great deal for a one day promotion for only $5.

2. www.freebookshub.com
This is another very inexpensive investment if you're tight on cash. Based on which promotion you choose, the investment for this website ranges between $10-$20 for a one day promotion. The numbers are about the same as BKnights on

Fiverr that I just shared with you. For only $10-$20 give this website a try and see how your books do.

3. www.bookmarketingtools.com
This website only does promotions for a free book giveaway. It costs $29 and allows you to submit your free book giveaway to over twenty-five different promotional websites. This means that on the day of your free book giveaway you will have twenty-five different book promotional websites driving traffic to your book. You should receive anywhere from 250-1,000 free downloads of your book on the date of your giveaway.

4. www.readingdeals.com
This website does both free and paid $0.99 book promotions, and the cost is $29. In order to use this website your book must have at least 5 customer reviews on Amazon. You

should average 250-1,000 downloads for a free promotion, and 15-30 sales for a paid promotion.

5. www.buckbooks.net

This website does both free and paid $0.99 book promotions, and the cost is $29. In order to use this website your book must have at least 10 customer reviews on Amazon. You should average 250-1,000 downloads for a free promotion, and 15-30 sales for a paid promotion.

6. www.manybooks.net

This website does both free and paid $0.99 book promotions, and the cost is $29. In order to use this website your book must have at least 10 customer reviews on Amazon. You should average 500-1,000 downloads for a free promotion, and 25-50 sales for a paid promotion.

The next few websites are a little bit more expensive. Again, you need to have vision and believe that your investment will come back to you.

7. www.ereadernewstoday.com
This website does both free and paid $0.99 book promotions. Based on which promotion you choose, the investment for this website ranges between $35-$135 for a one day promotion. In order to use this website your book must be at least 125 pages in length. You should average 500-1,000 downloads for a free promotion, and 25-50 sales for a paid promotion.

8. www.bookbub.com
This website has a huge platform for you. This website can absolutely get your book to the number one ranking in your category, at least for a day or two anyway. This website does both

free and paid $0.99 book promotions. The results you achieve from this website come with a GUARANTEE. This website offers a lot of different options. Based on which promotion you choose, the investment for this website will cost you anywhere between $250-$2,500 for a one day promotion. However, this website is very picky and rejects about 90% of the books submitted. This is one of the best book promotion websites out there for an author who doesn't have six figures to spend on book marketing. This website has launched many unknown authors to the number one best sellers list. Based on what category your book is in you should average 10,000-50,000 downloads for a free promotion, and 1,500-3,000 sales for a paid promotion. If you have the money to spend, and of course, if your book gets accepted, this website has the power to open a lot of doors for you as an author. Submit your books to them until you get accepted. It will be more than worth it.

9. https://advertising.amazon.com I've decided to save the very best for last. Well, in my opinion anyway. This marketing strategy is my absolute favorite and can make you a fortune. It's **Amazon Marketing Services**, also known as pay per click ads directly on Amazon. You can get started with this method by clicking on the link above or by logging into your Kindle account and click on **reports**.

As an author, Amazon Marketing Services is better for you than Google or Facebook ads. If you were to place a pay per click ad on either Google or Facebook two bad things will happen:

1. You will pay much more for your advertising costs than you will with Amazon Marketing Services.

2. You will have to convince someone to leave Google or Facebook to click over to Amazon. This loses sales.

You see, when people go to Google, they're searching for information. When people go to Facebook, they're wanting to connect with their friends and family. However, when people go to Amazon, they're looking to buy something. So, when you use Amazon Marketing Services to market your books to people with pay per click ads, the only people who see your ads are people who are actually looking for what you have to offer. This is called targeted traffic, which means sales, increased rankings for your books, and money in your pocket.

Investing in pay per click ads with Amazon Marketing Services in my opinion is the best investment an author can make in themselves. You can choose to invest as little or as much money as you want. Spending just a little bit of money can lead to a big return on your investment.

I run pay per click ads on Amazon and my returns on investments for some of my ads are over 1,100%. Try getting that kind of a return on your money from your bank, your real estate investments, or the stock market. If you start studying the proper way to create pay per click ads on Amazon, not only will you have a huge advantage over all the other wannabe authors out there, but you could literally make a fortune.

Amazon Marketing Services will provide you with all of the following benefits as an author:

-You can create targeted ads by shopper search keywords or phrases.

-You can create ads quickly and easily. You don't need any design or technical expertise to succeed.

-You can optimize the performance of your ads with detailed sales reports.

-You only pay when shoppers click on your ads.

In my personal opinion, and from the bottom of my heart, the best advice I can offer you in this book is to highly encourage you to become a master at pay per click ads using Amazon Marketing Services. It's very unknown to most authors and it's still in its infancy stage. If you get in now on the ground floor before the masses catch on, you could live off of the profits you bring in for the rest of your life. That's how huge of an opportunity this is. Don't take this time in history for granted. More and more people are getting downright wealthy from Amazon every single day. You could be next, but you must start taking action right now!

If you invest your money into any of the promotional websites that I just shared with you, then your books can definitely benefit from it. If you have several books that you've already published, then a free book giveaway promotion can definitely be a good thing for you. However, if you're a brand new author with only one book to promote, I would definitely do the paid $0.99 book promotion instead. This is a much better option for you until you have several books that can be cross promoted to buyers.

Each website has different time periods in which they can get to your books. So, I recommend that you submit your books to them a week ahead of the date that you actually want your promotions to start. I encourage you to use all of these websites and track your results from each one. Come up with a personal system for each book that you publish and remember that the most important thing is to be consistent.

After you read this book, would you mind doing me a huge favor please? Would you be kind enough to write me a five star customer review for this book on Amazon? By giving this book a good review it will help me as an author and help this book move up the rankings on Amazon. Your words have power. If you wouldn't mind supporting this book, I would be extremely grateful. I would love to hear your feedback. You're welcome to contact me at me personal website anytime. I wish you the very best of success in every area of your life!

Sincerely,
Christopher Mitchell
www.ChangeYourLifeOvernight.com

If you enjoyed reading this book, here's more books by the author:

-Sell Your First Book

-Vision Board Success

-Faith Produces Miracles

-My Inspiring True-Life Story

-Money Meditation Manifestation

-Why You're Fat & Sick And How To Fix It

-How To Lose Weight With Intermittent Fasting

-Network Marketing Success, Failure, & Everything In Between

-Success: The Secret To Becoming Happy, Healthy, And Wealthy

All books can be purchased from:
www.amazon.com/author/fitchristophermitchell